Way of Life

Dr Imhotep James

A New Way of Life

Authored by Dr Imhotep James

© Dr Imhotep James **2024**

Cover Design: Blonde Precious Dragon Blake / Marcus Tennant.

Proofread by Marcia M Publishing House Editorial team

All rights reserved 2024 Dr Imhotep James

www.marciampublishing.com

Table of Contents

Herbal Dictionary

Growing up in the warm tropical country of Jamaica, I've observed various herbs heal and cure ailments with simple, everyday household seasoning and spices.

Listed below are a few of the most important ones I've learned about and their uses. The secret to successfully administering these remedies is to keep consistent in drinking the teas every day until the symptoms subside.

Add 1 teaspoon of crushed herb to 1 cup of boiling water, cover and let sit for 5-7 minutes. Strain off the herb and drink the liquid as warm as you can take it.

For roots and barks, simmer 1 teaspoon in 1 cup of water for 5-10 minutes then turn off the flame, cover and let sit for 5 minutes, strain and drink as warm as you can bear it. Sweeten with honey if desired.

AFRICAN BLACK SPICE - *Xylopia aethiopica*

AFRICAN BLACK SPICE -;	FLAVOURING DYSENTERY DIARRHOEA RHEUMATISM FACILITATES CHILDBIRTH MORNING SICKNESS

AFRICAN CAYENNE - *Capsicum annuum*

AFRICAN CAYENNE -	CIRCULATION REMOVES MUCUS WARMS BODY UNCLOGS ARTERIES AIDS IN DIGESTION REDUCES THE RISK OF HEART ATTACKS

AFRICAN EYEBRIGHT - *Euphrasia officinale*

AFRICAN EYEBRIGHT -	NOURISHING EYES HAY FEVER IMPROVES VISION ALLERGIES INFLAMMATION OF NASAL CAVITY SINUSITIS ANTIBIOTIC PROPERTIES

AFRICAN GINGER - *Siphonochilus aethiopicus*

AFRICAN GINGER -	STOMACH DIGESTION MUSCLE RELAXANT CLEANSES RESPIRATORY GLANDS HAS ANTIBIOTIC PROPERTIES

AFRICAN MAHOGANY BARK - *Khaya ivorensis*

AFRICAN MAHOGANY BARK -	MALE REPRODUCTIVE ORGANS INFERTILITY IN WOMEN BODY WEAKNESS (especially in your back, waist and legs)

ALLIGATOR PEPPER - *Aframomum melegueta*

ALLIGATOR PEPPER -	CHEW SEEDS FOR ENERGY RELIEVES GAS AIDS INDIGESTION RELIEVES CRAMPS

AVOCADO LEAF - *Persea americana*

AVOCADO LEAVES -	NERVES MUCUS KIDNEYS HIGH BLOOD PRESSURE ENHANCES BLOOD CIRCULATION BONE-ENHANCING CALCIUM

BLUE VERVAIN- *Verbena hastata*

| BLUE VERVAIN - | HEADACHES FEVERS COUGHS SKIN WOUNDS BOOSTS LACTATION CALMS NERVES AND MOOD SWINGS KIDNEY AND LIVER DETOXIFICATION |

BLACK SEED- *Nigella sativa*

| BLACK SEED - | BOOSTS IMMUNE SYSTEM FIGHTS CANCER BAD BREATH RINGWORMS RELIEVES GAS AND INDIGESTION MENSTRUAL CRAMPS COVID-19 SYMPTOMS |

BLACK WISS - *Trichostigma octandrum*

| BLACK WISS - | REGULATES GLANDS INFLAMMATION CLEANS JOINTS SUPPLIES ENERGY |

BLOOD LEAF- *Iresine herbstii*

BLOOD LEAVES -   SUPPLIES IRON ANAEMIA
FOOD SUPPLEMENT
PROTECTS LIVER LOWERS
CHOLESTEROL POWERFUL
ANTIOXIDANT

BRAZIL WOOD - *Paubrasilla echinata*

BRAZIL WOOD -   DIABETES KIDNEY
PROBLEMS PANCREAS
SUSTAINS ERECTIONS
BOOSTS BLOOD
CIRCULATION INCREASES
SPERM VIABILITY HIGH
BLOOD PRESSURE
URINARY PROBLEMS

BREADFRUIT LEAF- *Artocarpus altilis*

BREADFRUIT LEAVES -   HIGH BLOOD PRESSURE
ARTHRITIS KIDNEY
PROBLEMS ASTHMA
BACK PAIN GOUT HIGH
BLOOD PRESSURE FEVER
LIVER DISEASE
TOOTHACHES

BRIAL WISS

BRIAL WISS –

BLOOD TONIC
STRENGTHENS BACK
BOOSTS LIBIDO AND SEX
DRIVE

BROOM WEED– *Gutierrezia sarothrae*

BROOM WEED –

USED TO BREAK UP
INFECTIONS IN BLADDER
AND REPRODUCTIVE
SYSTEM USEFUL AGAINST
VENEREAL DISEASE FOR
BURNING URINE BRINGS
DOWN FEVER (especially in
infants)

CAPADULLA

CAPADULLA –

IMPOTENCE
DISINFECTANT DIABETES
SORE EYES COUGHS

CERASEE - *Momordica charantia*

CERASEE -

DIABETES WORMS
MALARIA HYPERTENSION
DYSENTERY BLOOD
PURIFIER LOWERS BLOOD
SUGAR AND PRESSURE
RELIEVES CONSTIPATION

CHANEY ROOT- *Smilax Balbisiana*

CHANEY ROOT -

SKIN PROBLEMS SYPHILIS
RHEUMATISM AND
ARTHRITIS BALANCES
HORMONES BLOOD AND
DIGESTIVE CLEANSER

CINNAMON LEAF- *Cinnamomum verum*

CINNAMON LEAVES -

STOMACH PAINS COLDS
MUCUS CONGESTION
NOSEBLEEDS STIMULANT
FLAVOURING PAIN
RELIEVER

CLOVES- *Syzygium aromaticum*

CLOVES -	PAIN RELIEVER FOR CAVITIES HOARSENESS VOMITING RELIEVES GAS DISINFECTS STOMACH KILLS PARASITES FIGHTS CANCER

COCKSHUN - *Smilax Schomburgkiana*

COCKSHUN -	URINARY BLADDER IRON MALE TONIC NERVES SHRINKS FIBROIDS AND CYSTS PROSTATE CANCER

COCOA BALLS-*Theobroma cacao*

COCOA BALLS -	ENERGY DEPRESSION RELAXANT NERVES CHOLESTEROL REDUCES INFLAMMATION

COCONUT ROOT-*Cocos nucifera*

COCONUT ROOT -	EASES TOOTHACHE FEVER REDUCES BODY HEAT STOPS MENSTRUAL HAEMORRHAGING URINARY ISSUES

DAMIANA-*Turnera diffusa*

DAMIANA -   NERVES MENOPAUSE
                            HEADACHES ENERGIZES
                            MALES CONSTIPATION
                            APHRODISIAC

DANDELION LEAF- *Taraxacum officinale*

DANDELION LEAF -   ARTHRITIS RHEUMATISM
                            KIDNEYS BLOOD
                            PURIFIER NEUTRALIZES
                            ACID IN THE BODY

DEVIL'S HORSEWHIP-*Achyranthes aspera*

DEVIL'S HORSEWHIP -   COUGHS COLDS CHEST
                            PAINS COLIC FEVER
                            VENEREAL DISEASE SKIN
                            DISEASE INSECT
                            ALLERGY

DONKEY WEED - *Stylosanthes Hamata*

DONKEY WEED -   KIDNEY PAINS COLDS
                            ARTHRITIS DIZZINESS
                            TEETHING IN BABIES SKIN
                            PROBLEMS (warts and
                            moles)

FEVER GRASS - *Cymbopogon citratus*

FEVER GRASS -

FEVERS FLU AND COLDS
MALARIA COUGHS
PNEUMONIA HEADACHES
NERVES STOMACH AND
BOWEL PAINS

FOUR MAN'S STRENGTH - *Stermodia Maritima*

FOUR MAN'S
STRENGTH -

MALE AND FEMALE BODY
TONIC REPRODUCTIVE
ORGANS SPINE BODY
PAIN

GUAVA LEAF - *Psidium guajava*

GUAVA LEAVES -

BLOOD PRESSURE WORMS
NERVES DIABETES
MANAGE SUGAR LEVELS
FIGHTS CANCER
DIARRHOEA
CHOLESTEROL

GINKGO LEAF- *Ginkgo biloba*

GINGKO LEAVES -   IMPROVES MEMORY
CIRCULATION OF BLOOD
TO BRAIN AND
EXTREMITIES OF BODY,
FEET AND FINGERS, ALL
RESPIRATORY AND HEART
PROBLEMS

GOD BUSH - *Oryctanthus Occidentalis*

GOD BUSH LEAVES -   CENTRAL NERVOUS
SYSTEM INSOMNIA
(especially in infants)
LOWER BLOOD PRESSURE
ALL WOMB AILMENTS
BODILY PAINS

JACK IN THE BUSH - *Chromolaena odorata*

JACK IN THE BUSH -   COLD MEDICINE CALMS
NERVES RELIEVES
DEPRESSION COUGHS
NERVOUSNESS (especially in
children)

KING OF THE FOREST - *Cassia alata*

KING OF THE FOREST -   HYPERTENSION ASTHMA
THROAT PROBLEMS LIVER
SPOTS HERPES RASHES
LIVER KILLS PARASITES
BLADDER

KOLA NUT (BISSY) - *Cola acuminata*

KOLA NUT (BISSY) -   REGULATES HEARTBEAT
CHILLS ALL FOOD
POISONS DIARRHOEA
COLD SWEATS ENERGY
PROTECTS FROM VIRUSES

LEAF OF LIFE - *Bryophyllum pinnatum*

LEAF OF LIFE -   SHORTNESS OF BREATH
CHEST COLDS KIDNEY
FAILURE ASTHMA
MENSTRUAL PROBLEMS
ABSCESS CLEANS BLADDER
SINUS

MANGO LEAF - *Mangifera Indica*

MANGO LEAF -   KIDNEY STONES HIGH
                                 BLOOD PRESSURE
                                 RELATED TO NERVOUS
                                 CONDITIONS HAIR
                                 PROBLEMS GALL AND
                                 KIDNEY STONES

MARSH MARIGOLD - *Caltha palustris L.*

MARSH MARIGOLD -   LIVER AILMENTS
                                 HEPATITIS MENSTRUAL
                                 PAINS BRONCHITIS
                                 CRAMPS

MAUBY BARK - *Colubrina elliptica*

MAUBY BARK -   DIABETES ASTHMA HIGH
                                 BLOOD PRESSURE
                                 INSOMNIA DIARRHOEA
                                 STAMINA REDUCES
                                 SUGAR IN THE BLOOD

MEDINA - *Alysicarpus vaginalis*

MEDINA -	STRENGTHENS MALE REPRODUCTIVE ORGANS COMBATS ANAEMIA AND LOW BLOOD COUNT RELIEVES COLDS BOOSTS IMMUNITY AIDS DIGESTION BRAIN POWER

MILK WISS - *Foresteronia floribunda*

MILK WISS -	TUMOURS BOOSTS SEX DRIVE REMOVES MUCUS FROM THE BODY

MOJO BUSH - *Pittosporum tobira*

MOJO BUSH -	SKIN BLOOD CIRCULATION CLEANSER PURIFIER STIMULANT STOMACH AND INTESTINAL CLEANSER GALL BLADDER KILLS PARASITES

MONKEY LADDER - *Entada gigas*

MONKEY LADDER -	IMPOTENCE KIDNEYS STRENGTHENS MALE SEXUAL ORGANS

NASEBERRY LEAF - *Manikara zapot*

NASEBERRY LEAF -   NERVE TONIC COLDS
FEVERS DIARRHOEA
COUGHS

NEEM LEAF - *Azadirachta indica*

NEEM LEAVES -   COLDS ASTHMA CANCER
FEVERS BLOOD CLEANSER
CALMS BODY STIMULATES
IMMUNE SYSTEM HEALS
ULCERS

PEPPER ELDER - *Peperomia pellucida*

PEPPER ELDER -   IMPROVES CIRCULATION
STOMACH UTERUS CRAMPS
CONJUNCTIVITIS
GASTROINTESTINAL

PURON BARK - *Prunus occidentalis*

PURON BARK -   TONIC FOR THE ENTIRE
BODY ENERGY MALE
WEAKNESS CLEANS BLOOD
STRENGTHENS ORGANS
IMPOTENCE

PIMENTO LEAVES - *Pimenta dioica*

PIMENTO LEAVES -   STIMULANT DIABETES
                        STOMACH PAINS WORMS
                        PREVENTS STROKES
                        WARMS BLOOD AND
                        BODY REDUCES URGE
                        FOR TOBACCO

PURPLE SAGE - *Salvia leucophylia*

PURPLE SAGE -   COLDS CLEARS MUCUS
                        PMS MENOPAUSE
                        GINGIVITIS UPSET
                        STOMACHS

QUASSIA WOOD - *Quassia amara*

QUASSIA WOOD -   ALCOHOLISM LIVER
                        STOMACH COMPLAINTS
                        DIGESTIVE SYSTEM KILLS
                        LICE AND PARASITES

RAM GOAT DASH-ALONG - *Turnera Ulmifolia*

RAM GOAT DASH-   GOOD TONIC FOR COLDS
ALONG -   REMOVES MUCUS FROM
                        BODY EXPECTORANT HAIR
                        LOSS THRUSH

RA- MOON - *Trophies racemosa*

RA- MOON-   BODY BUILDER FERTILITY
                               INCREASES SPERM
                               COUNT ALLEVIATES
                               TIREDNESS AND FATIGUE

SARSAPARILLA - *Jamaican sarsaparilla*

SARSAPARILLA -   BLOOD CLEANSER
                               ECZEMA BALANCES
                               HORMONES PSORIASIS
                               REPRODUCTIVE ORGANS
                               SYPHILIS OTHER SKIN
                               CONDITIONS ALL
                               CHRONIC AILMENTS

SEARCH-MI-HEART -*Rhytidophyllum Tomentosum*

SEARCH-MI-HEART -   HEART ASTHMA MUCUS
                               CONGESTION STOMACH
                               PROBLEMS COLD AND
                               CHEST PROBLEMS
                               MENSTRUAL CRAMPS

SEMI-CONTRA (WORM GRASS)- *Epazote*

SEMI - CONTRA -

WORMS PARASITES
PALPITATIONS ASTHMA
STOMACH FEVERS
EXPECTORANT CATARACT
PROMOTES HEALTHY
HEART

SORREL - *Rumex acetosa*

SORREL -

IMPROVES EYESIGHT
PREVENTS CANCER
HEALTHY HAIR DETOXIFY
BODY WEIGHT LOSS
REDUCE COLD SORES
PREVENTS SCURVY
LOWER BLOOD PRESSURE
STRENGTHEN BONES
URINARY INFECTIONS

SOURSOP LEAVES- *Annona muricata*

SOURSOP LEAVES -

HIGH BLOOD PRESSURE
INSOMNIA GOUT FEVER
NERVE PROBLEMS KIDNEY
AND GALL BLADDER
PREVENTS CONSTIPATION

Nutritional Deficiency Diseases

Your body is your home.

At birth, we are given this fleshy avatar, and we learn to use it daily. From birth to death, you are responsible for your physical, mental and emotional health. Unfortunately, a baby doesn't come with a manual, so it is our prerogative to learn the dos and don'ts of everyday life. From nutrition to vaccination, you have to do what is right for your health, which is your wealth.

Poor nutrition contributes to stress, tiredness and fatigue, and affects our capacity to work. Over time it also can contribute to the risk of developing some illnesses or health issues such as being obese or overweight, tooth decay, high blood pressure and cancers.

Below are some examples of diseases that can result from nutritional deficiencies.

ACNE EFAs, Potassium, Vitamin A, Vitamin B-6, Zinc

ADD/ADHD Enzymes, Chromium, Vanadium

ANAEMIA Iron, Cobalt, Copper, Selenium, Biotin, Folic Acid, Nickel, Vitamin B-6, Vitamin B-12

ARTHRITIS Calcium, Copper, Boron, EFAs, Germanium, Glucosamine, AND Chondroitin Sulfates, Vitamin B6

ASTHMA EFAs, Magnesium, Manganese, Potassium, Zinc

BRITTLE

NAILS Calcium, Boron, Iodine, Iron, Zinc

CANCER Selenium, Germanium, Caesium, Antioxidants

CARDIOVASCULAR DISEASE Calcium, Copper, Vanadium

CHRONIC Biotin, Chromium, Copper, Iodine, Iron,

FATIGUE B-complex, Niacin, Selenium

CONSTIPATION Inositol, Iodine, Iron, Para-Amino Benzoic Acid, Potassium, Vitamin B-1, Vitamin B-12

DEPRESSION Biotin, Boron, Calcium, Chromium, Copper, Iodine, Iron, Lithium, B-complex, Zinc

DIABETES Chromium, Vanadium, Zinc

ECZEMA Boron, Calcium, EFAs, Inositol, Niacin, Vitamin B-5, Zinc

EDEMA Potassium, Vitamin B-1

GOITRE Iodine, Copper (low thyroid)

GREY HAIR Copper

HAIR LOSS Biotin, Copper, EFAs, Inositol, Iodine, B-complex,

HYPOTHERMIA Magnesium

LOW BLOOD SUGAR Chromium, Vanadium, Copper, Manganese

MEMORY LOSS Folic Acid, Niacin, Vitamin B-1, Zinc

NERVOUSNESS Calcium, Boron, Iodine, Magnesium, B-complex, Potassium, Vitamin D

OSTEOPOROSIS Calcium, Boron, Germanium, Vitamin K

PMS Calcium, Boron, Chromium, Zinc, Selenium

RECEDING GUMS Calcium, Magnesium, Boron

WRINKLES Copper, Sulphur

Nutrients And Vitamins Where Can We Get Them

Vitamins in their natural state give us the nutrients our bodies need.

Each one has a different job to keep the body working properly. They are essential for bodily functions such as helping to fight infection and healing wounds, making our bones strong and regulating hormones. While boosting immunity, they promote normal health and development.

Below are major vitamins, their functions and their sources.

VITAMIN A Helps with vision, tissue structure and immunity.

Source - Carrots, Dandelions, Greens, Mustard, Spinach, Apricots, Muskmelon, Papaya, Persimmons

VITAMIN C Antioxidant production of cells and organs, production of collagen, helps heart, bones and cardiovascular system, and enhances immunity.

Source - Broccoli, Brussels sprouts, Kale, Bell Peppers, Acerolas (acerolas are cherry-like with three lobes, bright red with thin skin)

VITAMIN D Helps the body use calcium and phosphorus for strong bones.

Source - Sunshine

VITAMIN E Powerful antioxidant power protects the heart, promotes slow ageing, protects skin.

Source - Leafy Vegetables

VITAMIN K Helps proper blood clotting and bone mineralization.

Source - Spinach

CALCIUM For your muscles to move and for nerves to carry between your brain and every part of your body.

Source - Alfalfa, Dandelion Greens, Leeks, Parsley, Spinach, Watercress, Almonds

MAGNESIUM Necessary for good nerve function, release of blood sugar, formation of cells.

Source - All green vegetables

POTASSIUM Maintains balance of water in body, helps prevent heart attack, needed for removals of toxins from cells.

Source - Bananas, apricots

SELENIUM Strong protective effect against cancer, helpful for heart help.

Source - Garlic, brewer's yeast

SODIUM Regulates water balance in the body

Source - Celery, Romaine Lettuce, Spinach, Bananas

CAROTENOIDS Protects vision, helps prevent heart disease and colorectal, lung and breast cancers.

Source - Carrots, Leafy Vegetables, Tomatoes, Apricots, Watermelon

FLAVONOIDS Cuts risk of mouth, throat and stomach cancers, defends against disease.

Source - Citrus Fruit

Ailments And
Herbal Remedies

Throughout my life as an herbal practitioner, I've guided folks from hell back to health using everyday plants and spices from right in your kitchen or garden.

Listed below are a few of the most important ones I've learned about and their uses. The secret to successfully administering these remedies is to keep consistent in drinking the teas every day until the symptoms subside.

Add 1 teaspoon of crushed herb to 1 cup of boiling water, cover and let sit for 5-7 minutes. Strain off the herb and drink the liquid as warm as you can take it.

For roots and barks, simmer 1 teaspoon in 1 cup of water for 5-10 minutes then turn off the flame, cover and let sit for 5 minutes, strain and drink it as warm as you can bear it. Sweeten with honey if desired.

COLON Aloe, Cascara sagrada, Psyllium husk

CONSTIPATION Senna leaves, Cascara sagrada, Barberry root, Aloe, Psyllium

CONVULSIONS Skullcap, Passion flower, Black Cohosh, Wild Lettuce

CRAMPS Blue Cohosh, Motherwort, Alligator pepper, Pepper elder

MENSTRUAL CRAMPS Blessed thistle, Strawberry leaves, Wild yam root, Dong Quai, Hops, Red Raspberry leaves, Ginger, Leaf of Life, White Jointa

DIABETES Bean pods, Blueberry leaves, Blue violet, Buchu leaves, Cat's claw, Goldenseal, China green tea, Juniper berries, Red Raspberry, Cerasse, Queen of the meadow, Mauby bark, Guava leaf, Pimento leaves, Taheebo, Trumpet Leaves, Periwinkle, Spanish needle, Fenugreek powder

DIGESTION Chicory root, Barberry root, Blessed thistle, Camomile, Hyssop, Horehound, Wheatgrass

DIZZINESS Camomile, Wood Betony

ECZEMA Aloe, Black Walnut, Cleavers, Oregon grape root, Straw-berry leaves

ENDURANCE Yohimbe, American Ginseng, Siberian Ginseng, Suma root, Astragalus root, Gotu Kola, Liquorice

EYES Blueberry leaves, Blue Cohosh, White willow bark, Plantain leaves

FEVER Bacopa, Boneset, Cleavers, Echinacea, Eucalyptus, Hops, Fenugreek seed, Passion flower, Red root, Rose hips, Strawberry leaves, Yellow dock, Mullein

FLU Fever grass, Peppermint, Soursop leaves, Shepherd's purse, White Jointa, Boneset, Catnip, Fenugreek seed, China green tea, Yarrow, Peppermint, Rose hips, Rosemary, Spearmint, Red clover, Red raspberry

GALL BLADDER Barberry root, Cascara sagrada, Dandelion root, Strawberry leaves, Milk thistle, Mojo bush, Soursop leaves

GALLSTONES Cascara sagrada, Dandelion root, Hyssop, Couch grass

GAS Peppermint, Ginger, Spearmint, Red sage, Blessed thistle, Sassafras, Blue vervain, Hyssop

FEMALE GLAND Angelica root

HAY FEVER Mullein leaves, Chickweed, Bayberry root

HEADACHES Camomile, Speedwell, Skullcap, Peppermint, Coltsfoot, Spearmint, Passion flower, Fenugreek seed, Wood betony, Rhubarb

HEART Hawthorn berries, Lily of the valley, Lobelia, Blueberry, Astragalus root, Search-mi-heart, Cat's claw, St John's wort, Kola nut, Horsetail grass, Rosehips, Lobelia

HAEMORRHOIDS Cascara sagrada, Aloe, White oak bark, Shepherd's purse

HAEMORRHAGE Bayberry root, Mullein leaves, Mistletoe, Nettle plantain, Periwinkle, Solomon seal, Shepherd's purse, Wild alum root, Yarrow

HIV Catuaba bark, Black seed

FEMALE HORMONES Black Cohosh, Blessed thistle, Dong Quai

HOT FLASHES Angelica root, Black Cohosh, Dandelion, Dong Quai, Passion flower

IMMUNE SYSTEM Black seed, Echinacea, Barley grass, Astragalus root, Cat's claw, Dandelion, Hibiscus, Suma root, Pau D'arco, Yohimbe bark

IMPOTENCE Catuaba bark

INFECTION Cat's claw, Echinacea, Myrrh, Rose hips

FEMALE INFERTILITY Chaste tree berries

INFLAMMATION Butcher's broom, Marshmallow, Mugwort, Slippery Elm bark

INSOMNIA Catnip, Camomile, Hibiscus, Kava kava, Passion flower, Peppermint, Skullcap, Valerian roots, Rooibos

ITCHING Chickweed, Goldenseal, Yellow dock, Plantain, Penny Royal, Barberry root, Chicory root, Milk thistle, Horny Goat, Mandrake root

JAUNDICE Cascara sagrada, Lungwort

KIDNEYS King of the forest, Barberry root, Bean pods, Cornsilk, Uva Ursi, Dandelion, Chicory root, Mugwort, Juniper Berries, Cleavers, Marshmallow, Plantain, Queen of the Meadow, Oregon Grape root, Sassafras, Trumpet leaves

LACTATION Blessed thistle, Marshmallow

LEUCORRHEA Black Walnut, Lady's Mantle, White Oak bark

LIVER Cascara Sagrada, Chicory root, Dandelion root, Milk thistle, Rhubarb root, Yellow dock, King of the forest, Neem leaf, Oregon Grape root, Mandrake

LUNGS Eucalyptus, Lungwort, Penny royal, Comfrey leaves, Shepherd's purse (milk this)

MENOPAUSE Angelica root, Damiana, Dong Quai, Chaste tree, Passion flower, Gotu Kola, Black Cohosh, Kelp, Valenan root

PAINFUL MENSTRUATION Chaste berries

REGULATE Angelica root, Blue cohosh, Penny royal, St John's wort,

MENSTRUATION Shepherd's purse

MENTAL CLARITY Bacopa monnieri, Gotu Kola

MORNING SICKNESS Alfalfa, Catnip, Peach leaves, Wild yam root, Raspberry leaves

NERVOUS SYSTEM Passion flower, Camomile, Peach leaves, St John's wort, Skullcap, Valerian root, God Bush, Trumpet leaf, Soursop leaf. Mango leaf, Rosemary, Strawberry leaves, Yerba mate, Hops, Catnip, Damiana

OBESITY Chickweed, Burdock root, Horsetail grass, Kelp, Sassafras

PAIN Camomile, Elderberries, Marshmallow, Lobelia, White willow bark, Wild yam root, Valerian root, Pau D'arco

PANCREAS Buchu leaves, Blue violet, Cascara sagrada

PITUITARY GLAND Alfalfa, Siberian ginseng, Gotu Kola, Kelp, Pygeum bark husk

POISON IVY Black Walnut, Mullein, Solomon Seal

PROSTATE Catuaba bark, Damiana, Siberian ginseng, Goldenseal, Corn milk, Juniper berries, Kelp, Saw Palmetto berries, Cat's claw

RHEUMATISM Blue flag root, Skullcap, Soapwort, White willow bark, Cat's claw, Burdock root, Devil's claw, Hydrangea root, Oregon grape root, Queen of the meadow, Chaney root, Red clover, Pau d'Arco

SEXUAL Catuaba, Damiana, American ginseng, Siberian ginseng,

STIMULANT Liquorice, Horney goat weed, Yohimbe bark

SINUS CONGESTION Bayberry root, Comfrey root, Eucalyptus, Fenugreek seed, Mullein, Rose hips

SKIN PROBLEMS Burdock root, Dandelion leaves, Dong Quai, Gotu Kola, Yarrow, Yellow Dock, Red clover, Sarsaparilla, Witch Hazel, Kwaku Bush, Soapwort, Chaney root

SORES Bayberry root, Black walnut, Kwaku bush, trumpet leaf, Solomon

UPSET STOMACH Chicory root, Lady's Mantle, Marigold, Quassia wood, Rhubarb root

SWELLING Chickweed, Comfrey leaves, Linden flower

SYPHILIS Blue flag root, Chaney root, Sarsaparilla

THYROID Black Cohosh, Kelp

REMOVES TOXINS Activated Charcoal, Blue violet, Yellow Dock root, Plantain leaves, Milk Wiss

TUMOURS Chaparral

URETHRAL IRRITATIONS Buchu leaves, Cornsilk, Uva Ursi, Wild yam root, Queen of the Meadow, Broomweed

UTERUS Aloe, Penny royal, Burdock root, Pau D'arco, Spikenard, Broomweed, Devil's horsewhip

VENEREAL DISEASE Yellow Dock

VITALITY Astragalus root, Burdock root, Dong Quai, Fo-ti powder, Liquorice, Gotu Kola, American ginseng, Siberian ginseng, Strawberry leaves, Suma root

WATER RETENTION Blue Cohosh, Uva Ursi. Burdock root, Butcher's broom Celery seed, Dandelion leaves, Hydrangea root, Couch grass

WORMS Semi-contra, Aloe, Black walnut, Camomile, Horehound, Red sage, St John's wort, Senna leaves, Solomon

WOUNDS Bayberry root, Chaparral, Comfrey leaves, Myrrh, Plantain leaves, Slippery Elm bark, Marigold

Eat enough food to meet your body's needs without leftovers for your hips and thighs.

Do not skip meals.

WATER Water, water, water – eight glasses a day

SALT Salt baths – Epsom salts Go to bed and perspire to promote circulation

Foods that protect you!

As we embark on this journey called life, daily emphasis is placed on the house we live in, the car that we drive, even the clothes we are attired in to look the best, to be the best on the outside. Yet, we chow down on three-tiered hamburgers made of meat made of God knows what, drink soft drinks and sodas made of tonnes of artificial colours and carbonated sweeteners. If you could see the damage done to your body by the fast and processed foods you consume every day, you would change your whole outlook on nutrition.

We have to focus on food items rich in vitamins and minerals. These are called **protective foods**. Although their micronutrients are required in small quantities; they are essential for maintaining a healthy body. Fruits and vegetables, especially dark, green, leafy vegetables should be consumed daily to obtain and utilize these vital micronutrients.

Below are some of the protective foods that can add to your overall nutrition and well-being, aid in improving your health and even reverse damage done by years of negligent consumption.

APRICOTS

- ❖ Combat cancer
- ❖ Control blood pressure
- ❖ Saves your eyesight
- ❖ Shield against Alzheimer's
- ❖ Slow ageing process

ARTICHOKES

- ❖ Aid digestion
- ❖ Lower cholesterol
- ❖ Protect your heart
- ❖ Stabilize blood sugar
- ❖ Guard against liver disease

AVOCADOS

- ❖ Battle diabetes

- ❖ Lower cholesterol
- ❖ Help stops strokes
- ❖ Control blood pressure
- ❖ Smooth skin

BANANAS

- ❖ Protect your heart
- ❖ Quieten a cough
- ❖ Strengthen bones
- ❖ Control blood pressure
- ❖ Block diarrhoea

BEANS

- ❖ Prevent constipation
- ❖ Help haemorrhoids
- ❖ Lower cholesterol
- ❖ Combat cancer
- ❖ Stabilize blood sugar

BEETS

- ❖ Control blood pressure
- ❖ Combat cancer
- ❖ Strengthen bones
- ❖ Protect your heart
- ❖ Aid weight loss

BLUEBERRIES

- ❖ Combat cancer
- ❖ Protect your heart
- ❖ Stabilize blood sugar
- ❖ Boost memory
- ❖ Prevent constipation

BROCCOLI

- ❖ Strengthen bones
- ❖ Save eyesight
- ❖ Combat cancer
- ❖ Protect your heart
- ❖ Control blood pressure

CABBAGE

- ❖ Combats cancer
- ❖ Prevents constipation
- ❖ Promotes weight loss
- ❖ Protects your heart
- ❖ Helps haemorrhoids

CANTALOUPE

- ❖ Saves eyesight
- ❖ Controls blood pressure
- ❖ Lowers cholesterol
- ❖ Combats cancer
- ❖ Supports immune system

CARROTS

- ❖ Save eyesight
- ❖ Protect your heart
- ❖ Prevent constipation
- ❖ Combat cancer
- ❖ Promote weight loss

CAULIFLOWER

- ❖ Protects against prostate cancer
- ❖ Combats breast cancer
- ❖ Strengthens bones
- ❖ Banishes bruises
- ❖ Guards against heart disease

CHERRIES

- ❖ Protect your heart
- ❖ Combat cancer
- ❖ End insomnia
- ❖ Slow ageing process
- ❖ Shield against Alzheimer's

CHESTNUTS

- ❖ Promote weight loss
- ❖ Protect your heart
- ❖ Lower cholesterol
- ❖ Combat cancer
- ❖ Control blood pressure

CHILLI PEPPERS

- ❖ Aid digestion
- ❖ Soothe sore throat
- ❖ Clear sinuses
- ❖ Combat cancer
- ❖ Boost immune system

FIGS

- ❖ Promote weight loss
- ❖ Help stop strokes
- ❖ Lower cholesterol
- ❖ Combat cancer
- ❖ Control blood pressure

FISH

- ❖ Protects your heart
- ❖ Boosts memory
- ❖ Lowers cholesterol
- ❖ Combats cancer
- ❖ Supports immune system

FLAX

- ❖ Aids digestion
- ❖ Battles diabetes
- ❖ Protects your heart
- ❖ Improves mental health
- ❖ Boosts immune system

GARLIC

- ❖ Lowers cholesterol
- ❖ Controls blood pressure
- ❖ Combats cancer
- ❖ Kills bacteria
- ❖ Fights fungus

GRAPEFRUIT

- ❖ Protects against heart attacks
- ❖ Promotes weight loss
- ❖ Helps stop strokes
- ❖ Combats prostate cancer
- ❖ Lowers cholesterol

GRAPES

- ❖ Save eyesight
- ❖ Conquer kidney stones
- ❖ Combat cancer
- ❖ Enhance blood flow
- ❖ Protect your heart

GREEN TEA

- ❖ Combats cancer
- ❖ Protects cancer
- ❖ Helps stop strokes
- ❖ Promotes weight loss
- ❖ Kills bacteria

HONEY

- ❖ Heals wounds
- ❖ Aids digestion
- ❖ Guards against ulcers
- ❖ Increases energy
- ❖ Fights allergies

JAMAICAN RED APPLE

- ❖ Protects your heart
- ❖ Prevents constipation
- ❖ Blocks diarrhoea
- ❖ Improves lung capacity
- ❖ Cushions joints

LEMONS

- ❖ Combats cancer
- ❖ Protects your heart
- ❖ Controls blood pressure
- ❖ Smooths skin
- ❖ Stops and prevents scurvy

LIMES

- ❖ Combat cancer
- ❖ Protect your heart
- ❖ Control blood pressure
- ❖ Smooth skin
- ❖ Stop and prevent scurvy

MANGOES

- ❖ Combat cancer
- ❖ Boost memory
- ❖ Regulate thyroid
- ❖ Aid digestion
- ❖ Shield against Alzheimer's

MUSHROOMS

- ❖ Control blood pressure
- ❖ Lower cholesterol
- ❖ Kill bacteria
- ❖ Combat cancer
- ❖ Strengthen bones

OATS

- ❖ Lower cholesterol
- ❖ Combat cancer
- ❖ Battle diabetes
- ❖ Prevent constipation
- ❖ Smooth skin

OLIVE OIL

- ❖ Protects your heart
- ❖ Promotes weight loss
- ❖ Combats cancer
- ❖ Battles diabetes
- ❖ Makes skin supple

ONIONS

- ❖ Reduce risk of heart attack
- ❖ Combat cancer
- ❖ Kill bacteria
- ❖ Lower cholesterol
- ❖ Fight fungus

ORANGES

- ❖ Build immune system
- ❖ Combat cancer
- ❖ Protect your heart
- ❖ Straighten respiration
- ❖ Prevent scurvy

PEACHES

- ❖ Prevent constipation
- ❖ Combat cancer
- ❖ Help stops strokes
- ❖ Aid digestion
- ❖ Help haemorrhoids

PEANUTS

- ❖ Protect against heart disease
- ❖ Promote weight loss
- ❖ Combat prostate cancer
- ❖ Lower cholesterol
- ❖ Aggravate diverticulitis

PINEAPPLE

- ❖ Strengthens bones
- ❖ Relieves colds
- ❖ Aids digestion
- ❖ Dissolves warts
- ❖ Blocks diarrhoea

PRUNES

- ❖ Slow ageing process
- ❖ Prevent constipation
- ❖ Boost memory
- ❖ Lower cholesterol
- ❖ Protect against heart disease

STRAWBERRIES

- ❖ Combat cancer
- ❖ Protect your heart
- ❖ Boost memory
- ❖ Calm stress
- ❖ Boost immunity

SWEET POTATOES

- ❖ Save your eyesight
- ❖ Promote gut health
- ❖ Lift mood
- ❖ Combat cancer
- ❖ Strengthen bones

TOMATOES

- ❖ Protect prostate
- ❖ Combat cancer
- ❖ Lower cholesterol
- ❖ Protect your heart
- ❖ Boost immune system

WALNUTS

- ❖ Lower cholesterol
- ❖ Combat cancer
- ❖ Boost memory
- ❖ Lift mood
- ❖ Protect against heart disease

WATER

- ❖ Cleanse urinary tract and bladder
- ❖ Promotes weight loss
- ❖ Combats cancer
- ❖ Conquers kidney stones
- ❖ Makes skin supple

WATERMELON

- ❖ Protects prostate
- ❖ Promotes weight loss
- ❖ Lowers cholesterol
- ❖ Helps stops strokes
- ❖ Controls blood pressure

RAW YOGURT

- ❖ Guards against ulcers
- ❖ Strengthen bones
- ❖ Lowers cholesterol
- ❖ Supports immune systems
- ❖ Aids digestion

Herbal Teas and Their Uses

From fighting a cold to a nice, relaxing brew, people all over the world have been drinking tea for thousands of centuries, and for good reason. Numerous studies have shown that a variety of teas may boost your immune system, fight off inflammation and even ward off cancer and heart disease.

Put the kettle on. Below we will learn some of the helpful herbs used in making tea, and their uses.

- Alfalfa tea aids digestion

- Aniseed tea is a decongestant for nose and sinuses

- Blackcurrant tea stimulates taste buds

- Burdock root tea helps sciatica and rheumatoid arthritis

- Chicory tea normalizes liver function

- Cinnamon tea clears the brain and improves thought processes

- Cornsilk tea reduces pain of urinary infections

- Dandelion tea improves liver function and kidney function

- Fennel tea is good for the pancreas

- Fenugreek tea is good for colds, clogged ears and aching sinuses

- Hawthorn berry tea is energizing to the elderly

- Horehound tea helps loosen heavy mucus

- Juniper berry tea helps cystitis or bladder inflammation

- Liquorice tea is a good laxative

- Mate tea tones muscles, especially the smooth muscles of the heart

- Nettle tea increases blood pressure (avoid if you have high blood pressure)

➤ Orange flower tea is a sleep aid

➤ Parsley tea is a diuretic (causing increased passing of urine)

➤ Raspberry tea tightens, tones and strengthens the uterus

➤ Red clover tea is an inner cleanser

➤ Sage tea improves brain nourishment and is known as the "thinker's tea"

➤ Slippery Elm bark tea is a pain reliever

➤ Thyme tea relieves sore throat and colds

I am sure if I dig in my brain some more there are many more I can add to this list, so stay tuned for Part II and we will learn more about herbal teas and their uses.

Teas To Avoid

People may think all teas are beneficial to health, but you may want to steer clear of these varieties:

★ Detox teas made for fad diets that suggest you will lose weight quickly.

These teas often come filled with laxatives that can do more harm than good.

★ Fancy teas, coffees and lattes and drinks from your favourite chain store or cafe. While some of these drinks, such as a green tea latte, may appear healthy, they are loaded with sugar.

★ Trendy bubble teas that are also loaded with sugar, calories and carbs have little or no nutritional value.

★ Herbal teas that may potentially trigger allergies. Many herbal teas contain different types of fruits, herbs, spices and flowers that some people are allergic to. Read labels carefully before buying and consuming any new herbal tea.

Blood Purifiers

★ Barberry

★ Camomile

★ Chaparral

★ Chickweed

★ Chlorophyll

★ Echinacea

★ Hyssop

★ Liquorice

★ Red Clover

★ Sarsaparilla

★ Taheebo

★ Yellow Dock

★ Yarrow

★ Burdock

★ Cascara

★ Sagada

★ Dandelion

★ Oregon

★ Grape

★ Peach

★ Prickly Ash

★ Stillingia

★ Comfrey

How To Slow Down Ageing

You are what you eat. Your body is your temple and has to be adored and worshipped.

Our duty to ourselves is to eat our way back to good health. Firstly, what one has to do is to purify the blood. To purify means to clean out.

How to put ageing on hold?

> ➢ Eat at least five to nine servings of fruit and vegetables a day.

A serving is one half cup of cooked or chopped raw fruit or vegetables; one cup of raw leafy vegetables, one medium piece of fruit or 6 ounces of fruit juice or vegetable juice.

➤ Eat lots of different fruits and vegetables because scientists don't know yet which might be the most powerfully protective method to prevent ageing.

➤ Choose fresh and frozen fruits over canned ones when possible.

➤ Drink both fresh fruits and vegetables juices because the extracted juices contain anti-ageing substances.

However, you can buy high-powered blenders that crush the entire fruit or vegetable, retaining everything, including the seeds and membranes in the citrus fruits. In that case, you get even more from the liquefied version.

➤ Eat vegetables, both raw and lightly cooked. Both have advantages. Raw foods are high in antioxidants, and cooking destroys them. In fact, light cooking boosts absorption of beta-carotene.

➤ Eat vegetables such as broccoli and cauliflower raw or lightly cooked and still crunchy, since heavy cooking destroys critical anti-ageing components, to get the most antioxidants. Choose deeply coloured fruits and vegetables. The darkest orange carrots, sweet potatoes and the deepest green leafy vegetables such as spinach and lettuces contain the most antioxidant arytenoids. Blueberries, because of the deep hues, contain a high concentration of antioxidants etc. Microwaving only destroys 15 per cent of vitamin C, and boiling destroys about 50 per cent. Steaming, grilling and stir frying are the best ways.

➢ Avocado is the master antioxidant.

➢ Blueberries, cranberries, strawberries, raspberries are loaded with antioxidants to save cells from premature ageing. Blueberries, for example, have more antioxidants called anthocyanins than any other food, and three times more than the richest sources: red wine and green tea. Blueberries and cranberries help ward off urinary tract infections, so when we eat all of these berries we mentioned here, as we get older we fight off cancer.

These are the anti-ageing potions. As we grow into the wisdom years, we need to consume these to alleviate damage made by our younger egos and at least postpone the inevitable destination.

Water Retention

❖ BLUE COHOSH
❖ BURDOCK

- ❖ CATNIP
- ❖ CORNSILK
- ❖ COUCH GRASS
- ❖ DANDELION
- ❖ FENNEL
- ❖ FENUGREEK
- ❖ GOLDENSEAL
- ❖ GOTU KOLA
- ❖ HAWTHORN
- ❖ HORSERADISH
- ❖ HORSETAIL
- ❖ HOPS
- ❖ JUNIPER
- ❖ PARSLEY
- ❖ PEACH BARK
- ❖ PLEURISY ROOT
- ❖ QUEEN OF THE MEADOW
- ❖ SAFFLOWER
- ❖ SLIPPERY ELM BARK
- ❖ ST JOHN'S WORT
- ❖ TAHEEBO
- ❖ UVA URSI
- ❖ WINTERGREEN
- ❖ YARROW
   FORMULAS: #3, #5, #19
   VITAMINS: B AND C

MINERALS: CALCIUM, POTASSIUM
 WOUNDS AND SORES

- ❖ ALOE VERA
- ❖ BAYBERRY
- ❖ BISTORT
- ❖ BURDOCK
- ❖ CAMOMILE
- ❖ CAYENNE
- ❖ CHAPARRAL
- ❖ CHICKWEED
- ❖ COMFREY
- ❖ DANDELION
- ❖ ECHINACEA
- ❖ GOLDENSEAL
- ❖ HORSERADISH
- ❖ HORSETAIL
- ❖ LOBELIA
- ❖ MYRRH
- ❖ PAPAYA
- ❖ PEACH BARK
- ❖ PLANTAIN
- ❖ SAGE
- ❖ SLIPPERY ELM BARK
- ❖ ST JOHN'S WORT
- ❖ TAHEEBO
- ❖ VALERIAN

- ❖ WHITE OAK BARK
- ❖ WILLOW
- ❖ WITCH HAZEL
- ❖ WOOD BETONY
- ❖ YARROW
- ❖ YUCCA
  FORMULAS: #4, #5, #26, #31
  VITAMINS: A, B, C, E
  MINERALS: CALCIUM
  YEAST INFECTION
- ❖ CAYENNE
- ❖ GARLIC
- ❖ WHITE OAK BARK
  FORMULAS: #32
  VITAMINS: A, C, E

Fresh garlic as a douche will usually clear up a yeast infection within three days. White oak bark may be added to the garlic for better results.

Fresh, homemade yogurt can be inserted in the vagina.

For babies, garlic water may be used to wash the affected area.

PRESSURE POINTS ON FEET

Where are the Foot Pressure Points?

There are multiple pressure points in the feet, and each is believed to have a corresponding area in the body that may benefit from distant pressure or massage.

Below is a list of foot pressure points, with the corresponding regions of the body these pressure points might be linked to.

PRESSURE POINTS	BODY REGION
Tips of the toes	Head and brain
Middle of the toes	Face and sinuses
Base of the toes	Teeth, gums and jaw
Base of the pinky toe	Neck
Outer side of the foot	Arms, elbows, knees, legs
Inner side of the foot	Neck, brain stem, thymus, spine
Bladder	
Outer side of ankle	Lower back
Inner side of ankle	Lymph glands, fallopian tubes, groin
Top, middle area of foot	Lungs, chest, breast, upper back

Different areas on the soles of the feet are associated with specific internal organs that cannot be accessed during massages, such as the kidneys, spleen and adrenal glands.

Below is a general breakdown of the pressure points and corresponding body areas:

➢ The top of the foot to the head

➢ The ball of the foot to the chest

➢ The arch area to the abdomen

➢ The heel of the foot to the pelvic area

Self-Massages to Try

You can try reflexology on common areas of the foot that respond to pressure. Try different locations, massages and amounts of pressure to notice a difference.

There are therapists who are trained in foot reflexology like me, but if you want to try massaging these areas on your own, apply pressure with a thumb or finger and then rub with small, concentrated movements. Foot reflexology should not cause pain, so don't push too hard. The pressure should feel similar to a foot massage. If there is pain, it is cause for concern.

Massage, pressure and other forms of stimulation can increase blood supply, improve circulation and help various substances move through the body. Sometimes referred to as a type of detoxification, reflexology is suspected to help remove calcium, lactate and uric acid buildup in your tissues, which can cause problems later in life.

Foot massages can aid as therapy for some health conditions, like:

➤ Sleep problems

➤ Migraines

➤ Chronic Pain

➤ Injury and illness recovery

➤ Stress management

➤ Diabetic neuropathy

➤ Multiple sclerosis

Pregnant women or those sensitive to overstimulation should avoid reflexology due to potential complications.

Kwanzaa Recipe

Benne Cakes

Benne cakes are a food from West Africa. Benne means sesame seeds. The sesame seeds are eaten for good luck. This treat is still eaten in some parts of the American South.

(Warning: Cookies and baking sheet will get very hot and can burn!

Always bake with a grown-up for help and safety!)

You will need:

- Oil to grease cookie sheet
- 1 cup finely packed brown sugar
- ¼ cup butter or margarine (room temperature)

- 1 egg (whisked)
- ½ teaspoon freshly squeezed lemon juice
- ½ teaspoon vanilla extract
- ½ cup all-purpose flour
- ½ teaspoon baking powder
- ¼ teaspoon salt
- 1 cup toasted sesame seeds

Preheat the oven to 325. Lightly oil a cookie sheet.

Mix together the brown sugar and butter and beat until they are creamy.

Stir in the egg, vanilla extract and lemon juice.

Add flour, baking powder, salt and sesame seeds.

Drop heaped and rounded teaspoons onto the cookie sheet 2 inches apart.

Bake for 15 minutes or until the edges are browned.

Enjoy!

Shiitake Mushrooms

Okay guys! Back to the educational stuff.

Another food that should be added to your daily diet is shiitake mushrooms. These mushrooms are rich in polysaccharides and beta-glucans. These compounds protect against cell damage and help your immune system by boosting white blood cell production for fighting off microbes. Polysaccharides also have anti- inflammatory properties. Below are six nutritional benefits of shiitake mushrooms:

❖ **Reduces Cholesterol**

A Swedish study has shown that shiitake mushrooms can effectively reduce cholesterol in the body. This ability is due to a compound called eritadenine, which can be found in shiitake mushrooms and its extract. Another study conducted in Japan showed that regular consumption of shiitake mushrooms increased the levels of cholesterol in the faeces, which means that less cholesterol is left over in the body.

❖ **Strengthens Immune System**

Another reason to eat shiitake mushrooms regularly is that they effectively strengthen your immune system. Shiitake mushrooms contain a powerful compound called lentinan, which enables your immune system to fight diseases and infections more efficiently. In fact, these mushrooms are believed to be more effective than many prescribed drugs. Shiitake mushrooms can help you battle more common infections like influenza to more serious health ailments like HIV.

❖ **Prevents Cancer**

The compound lentinan not only helps boost your immune system but can also help prevent cancer. According to studies, lentinan promotes several anti-cancer activities. It can reduce the growth of cancerous cells and prevent the spread of existing ones. The compound also stimulates your immune system to release proteins and cells that destroy cancer cells. Gastric cancer in particular can be prevented by regular consumption of shiitake mushrooms.

❖ **Prevents Thrombosis**

Consuming shiitake mushroom oil has also been shown to effectively prevent thrombosis. This is a health condition that produces blood clots in your veins which leads to restricted blood flow. If you've ever gone on a long-haul flight where you had to sit for long periods of time without activity, then chances are you've experienced this disorder. Thrombosis usually occurs in the veins of the legs and can be quite painful. Shiitake mushrooms contain high levels of lenthionine, which prevents platelets from aggregating.

❖ **Rich In Iron**

Shiitake mushrooms are rich in iron, a mineral which is essential for maintaining good health. Iron improves the circulation of oxygen through your blood. As a result, oxygen and other nutrients are effectively supplied to your muscle cells, brain and other parts of the body. Iron is also used to treat anaemia, so if you are anaemic as a result of menstruation or pregnancy, make sure you incorporate plenty of shiitake mushrooms into your diet. Iron can also boost your energy level and prevent fatigue.

❖ **Aids in Weight Loss**

If you are currently trying to lose weight, shiitake mushrooms make a great diet food. Not only do they contain few calories, but they are also packed with plenty of dietary fibre. This fibre slows down digestion so you feel full for a longer period of time.

Forget-Me-Nots ...

BOOST SEX DRIVE

- ❖ Walnuts
- ❖ Peaches
- ❖ Almonds
- ❖ Pumpkin seeds
- ❖ Watermelon
- ❖ Ginger
- ❖ Avocados
- ❖ Berries

IRISH SEA MOSS

- ❖ Gets rid of waste, toxins and faecal matter backed up in your colon
- ❖ Cleanse often to prevent weight gain
- ❖ Digestive issues
- ❖ Bloating
- ❖ Constipation
- ❖ Symptoms from IBS

NECESSARY FRUITS AND USES

- ❖ **Strawberries** fight cancer and ageing

  Protection and prevention fruit. Strawberries contain the highest rate of antioxidants among the most important types of fruit. They also protect the body from the causes of cancer and the blockage of blood vessels.

- ❖ **Kiwis** increase bone mass

  Small but strong kiwi. This is a good source of potassium, magnesium and vitamin E as well as fibre. Its vitamin C content is twice that of an orange.

- ❖ **Bananas** boost energy

- ❖ **Watermelon** controls heart rate

  The most wonderful fruit that quenches thirst. Made up of 92 per cent water and contains a giant dose of glutathione that helps to strengthen the immune system. The other nutrients found in melons are that they contain vitamin C and potassium.

- ❖ **Cherries** calm nervous system

- ❖ **Grapes** relax blood vessels

- ❖ **Mangoes** prevent cancers

- ❖ **Oranges** protect skin and vision

Eating two to four oranges a day helps maintain health, prevents colds, lowers cholesterol, dissolves kidney stones and reduces the risk of colon cancer.

❖ **Pineapple** fights arthritis

Eat Fruit on An Empty Stomach

We all think that eating fruit means buying fruit, cutting it and then just eating it. It's not what you think it is. It is important to know how and when to eat fruit.

What is the correct way to eat fruit?

Fruit should be eaten on an empty stomach. If you eat fruits on an empty stomach, they will play a very important role in detoxifying your body and provide you with lots of energy for weight loss and other life activities.

Fruit is the most important food. Let's say you ate two slices of bread and then ate a slice of fruit. The fruit slice is ready to go straight from the stomach to the intestines, but has been stopped. Why? Because you ate the bread before the fruit. Meanwhile, all the bread and fruit will rot and ferment and turn to acid.

So please eat the fruit on an empty stomach or before meals.

Have you ever heard people complain that every time they eat watermelon, they burp, or eating the fruit makes their stomachs bloat? Even when they're eating bananas, they feel like going to the bathroom, etc? Actually, all these problems will NOT occur if you eat fruit on an empty stomach. Because if you eat the fruit on a full stomach, it will mix with other foods that are already being digested and produce gas, and you will feel bloated.

You won't have tremors, baldness, anger and dark circles if you eat fruit on an empty stomach because all fruits become alkaline within our bodies. If you control the correct way to eat fruits, you will have the secret of beauty, longevity, health, energy, happiness and normal weight.

When you want to drink fruit juice, drink only fresh fruit juice, not from cans, bags or bottles. Do not drink juice that has been heated. Don't eat cooked fruit, because you won't get the most beneficial nutrients. Cooking destroys vitamins. But eating whole fruit is better than drinking juice. If you want to drink fresh fruit juice, let the juice mix with your saliva before swallowing.

You can only eat fruit for three days to cleanse or detoxify the body. Just eat fruit and drink fresh fruit juice over the course of three days and you will be surprised and your friends will be amazed.

Guava and papaya deserve the highest awards for containing vitamin C. Guava is also rich in fibre, which prevents constipation. Papaya is rich in carotene and is excellent for the eyes.

Scriptures That Encourage Health

Genesis 1:29

"And God said, Behold I have given you every herb bearing seed, which is upon the face of all the earth, and every tree, in the which is the fruit of a tree yielding seed; to you it shall be meat"

1 Corinthians 10:31

"Whether therefore ye eat or drink or whatsoever ye do, do all to the glory of God"

Revelation 22:2

"In the midst of the street of it, and on either side of the river, was there the tree of life, which bore twelve manners of fruits, and yielded her fruit every month: and the leaves of the tree were for the healing of the nations.

Acknowledgements

Dedicated to my family and friends

Inspired by my loyal clients

Dr John Henrick Clarke

Gregg Braden

Dr Yosef Ben-Jochannan

Darien Grindley

Atasha Williams

And my grandmother ... The one who started the herbal lifestyle quests. Thank you for your love and knowledge.

Love you, Grandma!

www.marciampublishing.com

Printed in Great Britain
by Amazon

58691581R00046